Winning Grants for Fire, Police, and Local Government

Real-World Strategies for Securing Over $5 Million in Public Safety Funding

Walter Amedee

This book is intended for educational purposes only. While every effort has been made to ensure accuracy, the author makes no guarantees regarding the outcome of grant applications.

Printed in the United States of America.

ISBN: 979-8-9957423-0-2

Contents

How to Use This Book

This guide is organized to help readers understand both the strategic and practical aspects of grant writing.

Part I – Real-World Grant Success presents examples of grant-funded projects that demonstrate how grant funding can strengthen public safety and municipal services. These examples illustrate how real community needs can be translated into successful grant proposals.

Part II – The Grant Writing Process provides a step-by-step overview of how to identify funding opportunities, assess organizational readiness, develop program concepts, and prepare competitive grant proposals. Readers new to grant writing may find it helpful to read this section in sequence.

Part III – Practical Tools includes checklists, self-assessment tools, and organizational strategies that can help agencies develop more effective grant programs. These tools can be used as reference materials when preparing future grant applications.

Although every grant program has unique requirements, the principles discussed in this guide apply broadly to many types of funding opportunities. Readers may choose to read the book from beginning to end or refer to specific sections when working on a grant proposal.

The most important lesson throughout this guide is simple: successful grant programs begin with clearly defined community needs, strong organizational planning, and careful attention to the requirements of each funding opportunity.

Introduction

If you are reading this book, chances are you are curious about grants and how they work. Maybe you are a new analyst in local government looking for ways to bring additional funding into your agency. Perhaps you are starting a nonprofit organization and searching for financial support for your mission. Or maybe you are part of an established organization that wants to expand its programs but needs outside funding to make it happen.

No matter your situation, one thing is certain: grants can play an important role in helping organizations launch new programs, expand services, and address important community needs.

Over the course of my career, supported by practical experience and formal education in public administration, I have successfully written and managed grant applications and funding requests securing more than $5 million in funding to support fire, police, public works, and emergency management programs. These grants have supported projects for fire departments, police departments, and public works agencies, allowing local governments to implement programs and purchase equipment that might not have been possible through local funding alone.

Through this experience, I learned that successful grant writing is not about luck or complicated language. It is about understanding how funding agencies think, identifying real community needs, and presenting a clear and well-organized proposal that demonstrates how a program will make a measurable difference.

At first glance, the grant application process may seem difficult and confusing. Many people assume that grant writing requires special connections or insider knowledge. In reality, successful grant writing follows a logical process that anyone can learn with the right approach.

This guide is designed to provide a practical overview of that process.

It will walk you through the steps needed to identify funding opportunities, assess your organization's readiness for grant funding, develop a strong program concept, and write a competitive proposal.

Whether you are applying for your first grant or looking to improve your success rate, the goal of this guide is simple: to help you better understand the grant process and give you the tools needed to pursue funding opportunities with confidence.

Key Question: *What could your organization accomplish if funding was no longer the biggest barrier?*

For templates, tools, and narratives, visit: www.walteramedee.com/

About This Guide

This guide is designed to provide a practical introduction to grant writing for individuals working in local government, public safety agencies, nonprofit organizations, and community programs.

While many books focus on grant writing for nonprofit organizations, this guide places particular emphasis on how grants can support the work of fire departments, police agencies, public works departments, and emergency management programs. These organizations often face significant funding challenges while providing essential services to their communities.

Throughout this guide, readers will learn how to identify funding opportunities, evaluate whether a grant is a good fit for their organization, and develop a competitive proposal that clearly explains the need for a project and the benefits it will provide.

The book combines practical instruction with real-world examples drawn from more than two decades of experience in municipal government. These examples illustrate how grant funding can support equipment purchases, staffing programs, infrastructure improvements, and community safety initiatives.

Although every grant program has its own requirements, most successful grant proposals follow a similar process. This guide walks through that process step by step, covering topics such as:

- Identifying community needs
- Developing a strong program concept
- Researching funding opportunities
- Preparing the key components of a grant proposal

- Managing grants after they are awarded

In addition to the technical aspects of grant writing, the guide also discusses how organizations can develop internal processes to evaluate funding opportunities and coordinate grant activities across departments.

Whether you are preparing your first grant application or looking to improve your success rate, the goal of this guide is simple: to help you better understand the grant process and pursue funding opportunities with confidence.

The techniques described in this guide are based on practical experience securing more than $5 million in grant funding supporting public safety and municipal programs.

Who This Book Is For

This guide is intended for individuals and organizations seeking practical guidance on how to identify and secure grant funding.

The information presented in this book is particularly useful for:

Local Government Staff: City managers, analysts, planners, and administrative staff who are responsible for identifying funding opportunities and supporting municipal programs.

Fire and Public Safety Agencies: Fire departments, emergency medical services agencies, and emergency management offices seeking funding for equipment, staffing, training, and preparedness initiatives.

Law Enforcement Agencies: Police departments and public safety organizations pursuing funding for crime prevention, traffic safety, community policing, and technology improvements.

Public Works and Infrastructure Programs: Departments responsible for transportation, environmental programs, and infrastructure projects that may benefit from state or federal funding opportunities.

Nonprofit Organizations: Community-based organizations and nonprofit groups looking to expand services and develop programs that address important community needs.

Students and Emerging Professionals: Individuals studying public administration, emergency management, nonprofit management, or public policy who want to better understand how grant programs support public services.

While the examples in this guide focus primarily on public safety and municipal programs, the principles of grant writing discussed in this book can be applied to a wide variety of organizations and funding opportunities.

PART I: REAL-WORLD GRANT SUCCESS

Setting the Stage: National City in 1999

When I began working for the City of National City on June 1, 1999, the organization faced a number of operational and financial challenges that were common among many local governments at the time.

The National City Fire Department was operating with aging equipment and limited resources. Several fire apparatus had exceeded their recommended service life, and critical equipment was in need of replacement. Facilities required upgrades, and available funding was often insufficient to address long-term capital and operational needs.

Like many cities, National City was also navigating financial constraints, including a structural deficit that limited the ability to fund large-scale improvements through local revenue alone. As a result, many essential needs remained unmet or were deferred.

At the same time, expectations for public safety services continued to grow. The community relied on the Fire Department, Police Department, and Public Works Department to deliver reliable and effective services, despite the limitations in available resources.

These conditions created a clear need for alternative funding sources.

Over time, grant funding became an important tool for addressing these challenges. By identifying opportunities and developing competitive proposals, the City was able to secure funding for staffing, equipment, apparatus, and public safety programs.

The following sections highlight examples of how grant funding was used to support these efforts and improve services for the community, including the Department's rise from Class 4 to Class 1 ISO rating.

Real-World Grant Success

Throughout my career in municipal government, I have had the opportunity to write grant applications supporting fire, police, public works, and emergency management programs. The following examples illustrate several successful grant projects and demonstrate how grant funding can help communities improve public safety and infrastructure. Each project addressed a different need, but all required careful planning, collaboration, and persistence.

SAFER Grant: Hiring Five Firefighters

One of the most impactful grants our department secured was through the federal Staffing for Adequate Fire and Emergency Response (SAFER) Grant Program, administered by the Federal Emergency Management Agency (FEMA). This program is designed to help fire departments increase staffing levels so they can respond more effectively to emergencies and reduce firefighter fatigue caused by excessive overtime.

At the time we applied for the grant, the National City Fire Department was experiencing significant staffing challenges. Several retirements and separations had occurred within a short period of time, leaving the department with fewer firefighters available for daily operations. In order to maintain minimum staffing levels, the department was frequently relying on overtime to fill vacant positions.

Operating with reduced staffing placed a significant strain on our firefighters. Long shifts and repeated overtime assignments can create fatigue and increase the risk of injury. In addition, reduced staffing levels can impact response times and limit a department's ability to meet national staffing standards for emergency response.

Through the SAFER program, the department requested funding to hire five full-time firefighters, with a total grant request of approximately $1.5 million over a three-year period. The goal was to restore adequate staffing levels, reduce reliance on overtime, and improve operational readiness.

The grant application required detailed information about the department's staffing levels, operating budget, call volume, and community characteristics. For example, the application documented that the department responded to more than 8,000 calls for service annually, including thousands of emergency medical incidents.

The grant was successfully awarded, allowing the department to hire five additional firefighters. These new positions helped stabilize daily staffing levels, reduce overtime demands, and improve the department's ability to respond to emergencies throughout the city.

However, receiving the grant was only the beginning of the work. SAFER grants are structured as reimbursement grants, meaning that the city must initially pay the firefighters' salaries and benefits and then submit documentation to FEMA for reimbursement.

For this grant, the reimbursement process required monthly payroll documentation for all five firefighters over the three-year grant period. Maintaining accurate records and submitting timely reimbursement requests required consistent coordination between fire department staff, city finance personnel, and federal grant administrators.

During the grant period, one firefighter did not successfully complete probation, which created an unexpected challenge. Because reimbursement was tied to active positions, the department had to delay reimbursement until a replacement firefighter was hired. The time between the vacancy and the new hire could not be recovered under the grant program.

Despite these challenges, the SAFER grant provided tremendous value to the community. The additional firefighters improved response capabilities, reduced stress on existing personnel, and helped ensure that the department could continue providing a high level of emergency service.

This experience also reinforced an important lesson about grant funding. Writing a successful proposal is only part of the process. Managing the grant after the award often requires just as much effort. Organizations pursuing grant funding must be prepared to invest time and resources not only in securing the grant, but also in managing the reporting, compliance, and administrative responsibilities that follow.

When managed successfully, however, grants like SAFER can provide transformative benefits for public safety agencies and the communities they serve.

Modernizing Fire Department Equipment Through Federal Grants

One of the most consistent uses of grant funding in the fire service is replacing aging equipment that can no longer meet modern safety and operational standards. Over several years, our department was able to secure multiple federal grants through the Assistance to Firefighters Grant (AFG) Program, which allowed us to modernize critical firefighting equipment and improve firefighter safety.

Like many municipal fire departments, the National City Fire Department operates with limited funding and must balance many competing priorities. Fire apparatus, communications systems, and safety equipment are essential to emergency response, yet these items are also extremely expensive to replace through local budgets alone.

One of the earliest grants we secured funded the purchase of a new pumper fire apparatus valued at approximately $280,000. The new engine replaced an aging unit that had accumulated high mileage and increasing maintenance costs. Older fire apparatus can become unreliable and may not meet modern safety and operational standards. The new engine provided improved reliability and allowed firefighters to respond more safely to both structural and wildland fires throughout the region.

In a later grant cycle, the department secured $248,456 through the

Assistance to Firefighters Grant Program toward the purchase of a Pierce Arrow XT 105-foot Quint aerial fire truck valued at $953,669. The existing aerial truck had been responding to more than 1,200 calls per year and was beginning to experience increased maintenance problems. The new apparatus significantly improved the department's ability to conduct rescues, ventilate structures, and fight fires in multi-story buildings.

In addition to fire apparatus, the department also secured funding to improve firefighter safety equipment. Through another Assistance to Firefighters Grant, the department received $104,651 in federal funding, combined with a city match of $26,162, to purchase 23 new self-contained breathing apparatus (SCBA) for firefighters. These breathing systems are critical for protecting firefighters from smoke, toxic gases, and oxygen deficient environments during interior firefighting operations.

Another grant helped upgrade the department's communications systems by funding mobile and portable radios valued at $143,487. Reliable communications equipment is essential during emergency incidents, allowing firefighters to coordinate operations, maintain situational awareness, and operate safely during complex responses.

Each of these grants addressed a different aspect of the department's operational needs, including apparatus reliability, firefighter safety, and communication capabilities. Together, they demonstrate how strategic grant writing can significantly improve a department's ability to protect its community.

These projects also illustrate an important lesson for grant writers working in public safety. Large improvements rarely occur through a single grant. Instead, progress is often made incrementally through multiple grant opportunities over time. By consistently identifying funding opportunities and submitting competitive proposals, departments can gradually modernize equipment and strengthen their operational capabilities.

For communities with limited local resources, programs such as the Assistance to Firefighters Grant provide an invaluable opportunity to enhance public safety and ensure that firefighters have the tools they need to protect lives and property.

Police Department Traffic Safety Grant

One of the most valuable lessons in grant writing is that successful projects often require collaboration across multiple departments. A good example of this occurred when I worked with the National City Police Department to secure a traffic safety grant aimed at reducing alcohol related crashes within the community.

The National City Police Department was awarded $301,143 in grant funding from the California Office of Traffic Safety, administered through the National Highway Traffic Safety Administration. The purpose of the grant was to reduce the number of people killed or injured in crashes involving alcohol or impaired drivers.

Traffic related injuries and fatalities are a serious public safety concern for many communities. Law enforcement agencies often rely on specialized enforcement strategies to deter impaired driving and identify dangerous drivers before tragedies occur.

The grant-funded a comprehensive DUI enforcement and awareness program. One of the key components of the program was the hiring of a full-time traffic enforcement officer. The grant covered 100% of the officer's salary during the first year and 50% during the second year, allowing the department to strengthen its traffic enforcement capabilities.

In addition to the staffing component, the grant-funded overtime operations for DUI and driver's license checkpoints and DUI saturation patrols. These enforcement strategies allowed officers to focus specifically on identifying impaired drivers and removing them from the roadway before accidents occurred.

The grant also funded important enforcement equipment, including a fully equipped police motorcycle, a Lidar speed measuring device, a Total Station for collision investigations, and supplies needed to conduct DUI checkpoints. These resources allowed the department to enhance its ability to detect unsafe driving behaviors and improve traffic safety enforcement.

Another innovative element of the program was the development of a "Hot Sheet" system that helped officers focus on repeat DUI offenders who were on probation or had suspended or revoked licenses. By identifying high risk individuals, officers were able to concentrate enforcement efforts where they were most likely to prevent future offenses.

Public awareness was also an important component of the program. DUI checkpoints and enforcement operations often generate media attention, which helps reinforce the message that impaired driving will not be tolerated. This increased visibility strengthens the overall deterrent effect and encourages safer driving behavior throughout the community.

For me personally, this project was particularly meaningful because it allowed me to work closely with the Police Department while still serving within the Fire Department. Through this collaboration, I became more involved in broader public safety initiatives and developed relationships with officers and leadership across departments.

The success of the project demonstrated that grant writing can play an important role in bringing departments together to address shared community challenges. It also reinforced the idea that grant opportunities should not be viewed as belonging to a single department. When agencies collaborate and share ideas, they can often identify funding opportunities that benefit the entire community.

This experience ultimately helped expand my role in the city's emergency management efforts and contributed to my being considered the city's Emergency Manager.

Public Works Equipment Grant

Not all grant opportunities are discovered through formal research databases. In some cases, they arise through simple conversations and collaboration within an organization.

One such opportunity occurred while I was working in municipal government and came across a grant program offered by the California Air Resources Board that supported the purchase of low polluting construction equipment for public agencies.

Although the grant appeared to be a good opportunity, I knew it would only be successful if it addressed a real operational need within the city. Rather than assuming it was a good fit, I approached the Director of Public Works and asked a simple question: whether the department had a grant writer and if the program might be useful to them.

The response was immediate. The department did not have a grant writer and was very interested in the opportunity.

After discussing the program requirements, it became clear that the grant aligned perfectly with the department's equipment needs. The program would allow the city to replace older construction equipment with newer, low emission models that were more environmentally friendly and more efficient for daily operations.

The grant program required agencies to purchase new equipment and scrap older equipment in order to reduce emissions from construction machinery. It was also a reimbursable grant, meaning the city would first purchase the equipment and then request reimbursement from the state.

The proposal requested $394,650 in grant funding toward the purchase of $496,769 in construction equipment, with the city providing $102,119 in matching funds. The equipment included construction tractors, a roller, backhoe, loader, and grader used by the Public Works Department to maintain streets and infrastructure throughout the city.

The grant application was successfully approved, allowing the Public Works Department to modernize its equipment while reducing emissions and improving operational efficiency.

Beyond the funding itself, this project was particularly rewarding because it demonstrated how grant writing can support multiple departments within a local government. By identifying opportunities outside my immediate area of responsibility and collaborating with another department, the city was able to secure funding that directly improved infrastructure operations.

The success of this grant also reinforced an important lesson: grant writers should never limit their focus to a single department or program area. Opportunities often exist across an entire organization, and simply asking the right questions can uncover needs that might otherwise go unaddressed.

Personally, the success of this grant also had a meaningful impact on my career. The project demonstrated the value that grant writing could bring to the organization and contributed to my receiving a promotion and salary increase.

This experience serves as a reminder that grant writing is not only about securing funding. It is also about building relationships, identifying opportunities, and helping organizations improve services for the communities they serve.

Emergency Operations Center Upgrade Grant

Effective emergency management requires more than trained personnel and response plans. It also depends on having the right facilities and technology in place to coordinate complex incidents. One important project that helped strengthen our city's emergency preparedness involved upgrading the Emergency Operations Center (EOC) through a grant provided by the San Diego Regional Fire Foundation.

Emergency Operations Centers serve as the central coordination point during major incidents such as large fires, severe weather events, earthquakes, and other disasters. During these situations, representatives from multiple departments and agencies come together to share information, coordinate resources, and make critical decisions that affect public safety.

Although the city had an established Emergency Operations Center, some of the technology used to support emergency coordination had become outdated. Communication systems, display capabilities, and information sharing tools needed improvement in order to support modern emergency management operations.

Through collaboration with the San Diego Regional Fire Foundation, the city secured approximately $82,222 in grant funding to upgrade key components of the Emergency Operations Center. The project focused on improving audio visual systems and communications technology used during emergency activations.

These upgrades significantly improved the ability of city leadership and emergency responders to share real time information during incidents. Modern display systems allow staff to monitor multiple information sources simultaneously, including incident maps, weather data, and operational updates from field personnel.

Improved communication capabilities also make it easier for departments such as fire, police, public works, and emergency management to coordinate response efforts. When agencies have access to the same information in real time, they are able to make faster and more informed decisions during rapidly evolving emergencies.

Projects like this are sometimes overlooked because they focus on infrastructure rather than personnel or equipment. However, effective emergency coordination can have a tremendous impact during major incidents. A well-equipped Emergency Operations Center helps ensure that response agencies can work together efficiently and maintain situational awareness during critical events.

This grant also demonstrated the value of partnerships between local government agencies and nonprofit organizations that support public safety initiatives. By working together, the city and the San Diego Regional Fire Foundation were able to improve emergency preparedness and strengthen the community's ability to respond to disasters.

The project serves as a reminder that grant funding can support not only front-line responders, but also the systems and infrastructure that enable those responders to operate effectively.

These examples represent only a portion of the grants I have helped secure during my career in municipal government. Each grant required research, collaboration, and persistence. While every funding opportunity is different, the same basic principles apply: clearly define the need, develop a realistic solution, and be prepared to manage the grant responsibly after it is awarded.

Long-Term Impact of Grant Funding

Over time, the cumulative impact of equipment upgrades, staffing improvements, training, and operational enhancements can significantly strengthen a fire department's ability to protect its community.

One important measure of fire protection capability in the United States is the Insurance Services Office (ISO) Public Protection Classification, which evaluates fire departments based on emergency communications, firefighting resources, water supply, and community risk reduction programs.

During my career with the National City Fire Department, the organization made steady improvements in many of these areas. Through investments in personnel, modern fire apparatus, communications systems, training, and emergency preparedness programs, the department continued to strengthen its operational capabilities.

In 2025, those efforts were recognized when the National City Fire Department achieved a Class 1 ISO rating, the highest possible designation awarded by the Insurance Services Office. This distinction places the department among the top one percent of fire departments in the United States and reflects the department's strong commitment to fire protection and emergency response.

While many factors contribute to a fire department's ISO classification, improvements in staffing, equipment, communications, and training all play an important role. Grants that support these types of investments can therefore have long-term benefits that extend far beyond the original project.

For communities with limited local funding, grant programs can provide critical opportunities to strengthen emergency response capabilities and improve overall public safety.

Grant Portfolio Summary

The following table summarizes grant funding and related funding sources secured to support fire, police, public works, and emergency management operations. These investments contributed to improvements in staffing, equipment, infrastructure, and community preparedness.

This table summarizes major grant funding secured across multiple programs. Individual awards have been consolidated for clarity and to highlight overall funding impact.

Grant-Funded Projects Overview

Project / Program	Dept.	Funding Source	Category	Amount
Assistance to Firefighters Grants (AFG – Combined)	Fire	FEMA	Equipment & Safety	$600,671
SAFER Grant (Firefighter Staffing)	Fire	FEMA	Staffing	$1,518,729
Homeland Security Grants (SHSP/UASI – Combined)	Fire / Regional	DHS	Emergency Management	$299,689
Community Development Block Grants (CDBG – Combined)	Fire / EM	HUD	Infrastructure / EMS / Shelter	$1,896,720
Traffic Safety Programs	Police	CA OTS	Public Safety	$301,143
Public Works Equipment Grants	Public Works	CA Air Resources Board	Equipment	$394,650
Foundation & Regional Grants	Fire / Police	Various Foundations	Equipment / Programs	$158,853
Other State & Local Grants (Combined)	Multi-Dept	State / Local	Various	$1,574,538

Total Funding Secured $6,744,993

PART II: THE GRANT WRITING PROCESS

What Are Grants and How Are They Funded?

Most often, grants are financial awards provided by government agencies, corporations, or foundations to assist state and local governments, nonprofit organizations, educational institutions, and community-based programs. A grant is funding that a grantor has made available for a specific purpose, such as public safety improvements, community development programs, education initiatives, or disaster preparedness.

Grants are not "free money." Each grant program has strict eligibility requirements, program guidelines, and reporting obligations that must be followed by the organization receiving the funding. Grant opportunities are typically announced through a Request for Proposal (RFP), Notice of Funding Opportunity (NOFO), or Request for Applications (RFA). These announcements describe the purpose of the grant program, the amount of funding available, the eligible applicants, the time period of the grant, and the requirements for submitting an application.

When an organization receives a grant award, it enters into a formal agreement with the funding agency. This agreement outlines how the funds must be used, how the project will be evaluated, and what reporting requirements must be fulfilled during the life of the grant.

In general, grants are designed to support new initiatives, expand existing programs, or address specific community needs identified by the funding agency. While grants sometimes fund equipment, staffing, or infrastructure, those expenses must typically be tied directly to the project being proposed. For example, a grant program may fund new emergency response equipment, but only if it supports the goals of the specific grant program.

Government grants are funded through appropriations made by Congress, state legislatures, or local governments. These funds are then distributed through various agencies that administer grant programs aligned with national or regional priorities. Government grants are highly competitive and are only available during specific application periods with strict deadlines.

One well known example in the public safety field is the Assistance to Firefighters Grant (AFG) program, administered by the Federal Emergency Management Agency (FEMA). Since its creation in 2001, the AFG program has provided billions of dollars in funding to fire departments and emergency medical services organizations to support equipment purchases, training, vehicles, and other critical resources needed to protect the public.

Another example is the Staffing for Adequate Fire and Emergency Response (SAFER) program, which provides funding to fire departments to help increase staffing levels and improve emergency response capabilities within their communities.

Corporate foundations also provide grant funding to support causes aligned with their corporate values or community interests. These grants often support areas such as education, youth development, environmental protection, or public safety. Corporate foundations may focus their giving within specific geographic areas where the company operates.

Private foundations are typically established by individuals or families who wish to support causes that are meaningful to them. These foundations often fund programs in areas such as education, health care, poverty reduction, and community development. A well-known example is the Bill and Melinda Gates Foundation, which supports initiatives related to global health, education, and poverty reduction.

According to the National Center for Charitable Statistics, there are more than 1.5 million nonprofit organizations in the United States. Many of these organizations rely on grants as an important source of funding to support programs that serve their communities.

Over the course of my career in municipal government, I have seen firsthand how grant funding can help agencies launch programs, purchase critical equipment, and expand services that would otherwise be impossible with local budgets alone. Understanding how grants are structured and how they are funded is the first step toward developing successful grant proposals.

Common Public Sector Grant Programs

Local governments have access to a wide variety of grant programs at the federal, state, and regional levels. While each program has its own requirements and priorities, several funding sources appear frequently in municipal grant programs.

The following examples represent some of the most common programs that support local government initiatives.

Community Development Block Grants (CDBG)

The Community Development Block Grant program, administered by the U.S. Department of Housing and Urban Development (HUD), provides funding to cities and counties to support community development projects.

CDBG funds are typically used for projects that benefit low- and moderate-income residents. Common uses include:

- Housing rehabilitation
- Neighborhood infrastructure improvements
- Community facilities
- Economic development programs

Many cities receive annual CDBG allocations and distribute the funds through local programs or competitive funding processes.

State Homeland Security Program (SHSP)

The State Homeland Security Program provides funding to states to support preparedness activities related to terrorism prevention, protection, response, and recovery.

These funds are typically distributed through state emergency management agencies and may support projects such as:

- Emergency response equipment
- Training and exercises
- Communications systems
- Regional planning initiatives

Local governments often access these funds through regional partnerships or state administered grant programs.

Urban Area Security Initiative (UASI)

The Urban Area Security Initiative is designed to enhance preparedness in high-risk urban areas. This program supports regional collaboration among multiple jurisdictions to improve the ability to prevent, respond to, and recover from major incidents.

UASI funding commonly supports:

- Interoperable communications systems
- Emergency operations center improvements
- Regional training exercises

- Specialized response equipment

These programs are often administered through regional governance structures that coordinate funding priorities among participating jurisdictions.

Congressionally Directed Spending (CDS)

Congressionally Directed Spending, sometimes referred to as earmarks, allows members of Congress to request federal funding for specific projects within their districts.

Local governments may pursue CDS funding for infrastructure improvements, public safety projects, or community facilities. These requests are typically submitted through a member of Congress during the federal appropriations process.

Because these requests are tied to the federal budget cycle, they often require early coordination with congressional offices and strong documentation demonstrating community need.

Understanding Funding Sources

While these programs represent only a small portion of available funding opportunities, they illustrate the variety of ways that local governments can obtain grant support for important projects.

Successful grant programs often involve monitoring multiple funding sources and identifying opportunities that align with the needs and priorities of the community. Grant programs evolve over time as federal and state priorities change. For this reason, grant writers should regularly monitor funding announcements and maintain communication with regional and state agencies that administer grant programs.

Choosing the Right Grant Opportunities

One of the most important decisions in the grant writing process is determining which funding opportunities are worth pursuing. While many grants are available through federal, state, and foundation programs, not every opportunity will be a good fit for every organization.

Key Question: *Is this grant a true match for our needs, or are we chasing funding?*

Successful grant programs often focus on projects that strengthen core capabilities, improve service delivery, or reduce risks within the community. Based on common public sector funding priorities, many municipal grant projects fall into three broad categories: life safety improvements, operational capability enhancements, and community risk reduction initiatives.

> **Grant Writing Tip:**
>
> *Not every grant is worth pursuing. Focus your time on opportunities that clearly align with your organization's needs and capabilities. A strong match between the project and the funding program is often more important than the size of the award.*

Life Safety Improvements

Life safety grants focus on protecting emergency responders and the public during emergency incidents. These grants typically fund equipment, personnel, or technology that directly improves the safety of first responders and the communities they serve.

Examples of life safety improvements may include:

- Firefighter protective equipment
- Self-contained breathing apparatus
- Communications systems used during emergency incidents
- Staffing programs that improve emergency response capability

Funding agencies frequently prioritize projects that improve life safety because these programs can have a direct impact on preventing injuries or fatalities.

Operational Capability Enhancements

Operational capability grants support projects that improve how agencies perform their daily responsibilities. These grants often fund equipment, vehicles, or programs that enhance the efficiency and effectiveness of public services.

Examples may include:

- Fire apparatus replacement
- Police enforcement equipment
- Public works construction or maintenance equipment
- Emergency response vehicles

Projects that improve operational capability are often attractive to funding agencies because they demonstrate measurable improvements in service delivery and operational performance.

Community Risk Reduction Initiatives

Community risk reduction grants focus on programs that help prevent emergencies or reduce their impact before they occur. These programs often emphasize education, prevention, and proactive safety measures.

Examples may include:

- Fire prevention education programs
- Traffic safety initiatives
- Disaster preparedness training
- Public awareness campaigns

Funding agencies frequently support these initiatives because they can reduce long-term costs associated with emergency incidents and improve overall community safety.

Selecting the Right Opportunity

Organizations that pursue grant opportunities aligned with these categories are often better positioned to develop competitive proposals. Projects that clearly demonstrate improvements in safety, operational capability, or risk reduction tend to align well with the priorities of many public sector grant programs.

Rather than pursuing every available funding opportunity, agencies should focus their efforts on grants that address clearly identified needs and support long-term improvements in service delivery.

Carefully selecting the right grant opportunities can help organizations invest their time and resources in applications that are more likely to succeed. Many successful municipal grant programs include a combination of projects that improve life safety, strengthen operational capability, and reduce risks within the community.

How Grant Opportunities Are Discovered

During my career in municipal government, I discovered that grant opportunities often arise in several different ways. While many people think of grant writing as simply searching for funding announcements, the reality is that opportunities are often identified through a combination of research, collaboration, and professional awareness.

Based on my experience, most grant opportunities tend to be discovered through three primary methods.

Direct Grant Research

The most traditional way to find grants is through direct research. This involves regularly reviewing grant announcements and funding opportunities from federal, state, and foundation sources.

Examples include:

- FEMA grant programs
- Department of Justice programs
- Department of Transportation safety grants
- State environmental or infrastructure grants

Many agencies publish funding opportunities through online portals, mailing lists, or professional networks. Grant writers who regularly monitor these sources are more likely to identify programs that match the needs of their organization.

Several of the federal fire service grants described earlier in this book were identified through this type of research.

Internal Conversations and Collaboration

Some of the best grant opportunities are discovered simply by talking with colleagues and learning about their operational challenges.

For example, one grant described earlier in this book involved equipment funding for the Public Works Department. The opportunity came to my attention while reviewing a grant program that supported low emission construction equipment.

Before pursuing the grant, I approached the Public Works Director to ask whether the department had a grant writer and whether the program might address a need within the department. The response was immediate. The department did not have a grant writer and was very interested in the opportunity.

By working together, we were able to submit a successful application that funded the replacement of several pieces of construction equipment used throughout the city.

This experience reinforced an important lesson: grant writers should look beyond their own department and explore opportunities across the entire organization.

Professional Awareness and Experience

Over time, experienced grant writers develop familiarity with recurring funding programs and emerging opportunities within their field.

For example, many fire departments are familiar with federal programs such as:

- Assistance to Firefighters Grants (AFG)
- Staffing for Adequate Fire and Emergency Response (SAFER)

Similarly, law enforcement agencies often pursue funding through traffic safety programs or Department of Justice grants.

Through experience, grant writers begin to recognize patterns in these programs, including when funding cycles typically occur and what types of projects are most competitive.

This professional awareness allows organizations to prepare projects in advance so they are ready to apply when funding opportunities become available.

The Key Lesson

Successful grant writing is not simply about completing applications. It also involves being attentive to opportunities, building relationships across departments, and maintaining awareness of funding programs that may benefit the organization.

Many of the grant successes described in this book began with a simple question:

- Is there a funding opportunity that could help us solve this problem?

By remaining curious and engaged with colleagues across an organization, grant writers can often identify opportunities that might otherwise go unnoticed.

Determining Need

Before seeking grant funding, an organization must clearly understand the problem or need it intends to address. Grant funders rarely support projects based solely on general ideas or assumptions. Instead, they expect applicants to demonstrate that a real and documented need exists within the community.

Key Question: *What specific problem are we trying to solve, and how do we* *prove it exists?*

Determining need is often the first step in developing a successful grant proposal. Organizations should begin by examining the challenges facing their community, the services currently being provided, and any gaps that may exist.

For local governments and public safety agencies, this process may involve reviewing information such as incident reports, service demand trends, community demographics, or strategic planning documents. These sources can help identify areas where additional resources, equipment, or programs may be necessary.

However, identifying a community need is only part of the process. Grant funders also want to know that the organization proposing the project has the experience, leadership, and capacity to address that need effectively.

For this reason, the next step in developing a strong grant proposal is understanding the organization itself and how it is positioned to carry out the proposed program.

Knowing Your Organization

Before preparing a grant proposal, it is important to have a clear understanding of the organization submitting the application. Grant funders want to know that the applicant has the experience, leadership, and organizational capacity necessary to successfully implement the proposed project.

Key Question: *Why is our organization the right one to carry out this project?*

Even if your organization is well known within the community, you should never assume that grant reviewers are familiar with it. In many cases, reviewers may be evaluating dozens or even hundreds of proposals, and they may have no prior knowledge of the organizations applying for funding.

For this reason, grant proposals typically include a brief description of the organization. This section helps establish credibility and demonstrates that the organization is capable of carrying out the proposed program.

When describing your organization, consider including information such as:

- The history of the organization
- The mission or purpose of the organization
- The population or community served
- The size of the organization and staffing structure
- The organization's experience managing similar programs
- Previous accomplishments or successful initiatives

For local government agencies, this section may also include information about the jurisdiction being served. For example, a city department may describe the population size, geographic area, and the types of services provided to the community.

Providing this background helps grant reviewers understand the context in which the proposed project will operate and why the organization is well positioned to carry it out.

It is often helpful to prepare a short organizational description that can be adapted and reused in multiple grant applications. Having this information readily available saves time when preparing proposals and ensures that consistent information is presented across different funding opportunities.

In addition to describing the organization's mission and history, grant funders are often interested in the organization's operational capacity. They want to know that the organization has the staff, systems, and financial oversight necessary to manage grant funds responsibly.

> **Grant Writing Tip:**
>
> *Many successful grant writers maintain a short organizational profile that can be reused and adapted for multiple grant proposals. Keeping this information updated can save time and ensure consistency across applications.*

This may include:

- Qualified leadership and program staff
- Financial management systems
- Experience managing grant-funded projects
- Partnerships with other organizations or agencies

Demonstrating organizational capacity reassures grant reviewers that the proposed project can be successfully implemented and sustained.

Ultimately, this section of the proposal should answer a simple question for the grant reviewer:

- Why is this organization the right one to carry out this project?

Your Proposed Program

Once you have identified a need within your organization or community, the next step is defining the program or project that will address that need. Grant funders want to see that applicants have a clear and realistic plan for how grant funds will be used to solve a specific problem.

At this stage, the goal is to clearly describe what your organization intends to accomplish. The proposed program should directly respond to the need you identified and should demonstrate how the project will produce measurable results.

For many organizations, the proposed program may already exist in some form and is seeking additional funding to expand or improve services. In other cases, the project may represent a new initiative designed to address a recently identified problem.

Key Question: *Can we clearly explain what we are doing, who it serves, and what will change?*

When developing a proposed program, consider the following questions:

- What problem or issue will the program address?
- Who will benefit from the program?
- What specific activities will take place?
- Who will be responsible for implementing the program?
- What resources will be required to carry out the project?
- What outcomes do you expect the program to achieve?

Clearly answering these questions helps ensure that the project is well defined before the grant proposal is written.

For example, a fire department may identify an increase in residential fires within certain neighborhoods. Based on this information, the department may develop a community fire prevention initiative that includes smoke alarm installations, public education campaigns, and home safety inspections.

Similarly, a police department may identify an increase in traffic related injuries and develop a traffic safety program that focuses on enforcement, public awareness campaigns, and community education.

Emergency management agencies may identify gaps in community preparedness and develop programs focused on disaster readiness training, emergency supply kit distribution, or community emergency response team (CERT) training.

Grant Writing Tip:

The most successful grant proposals begin with a clearly defined program concept. If you cannot explain your project in a few simple sentences, the proposal may need further planning before you begin writing.

By clearly defining the proposed program before writing the grant proposal, organizations can ensure that the project is practical, achievable, and aligned with the priorities of the funding agency.

A well-designed program also makes the proposal writing process much easier. When the program concept is clearly defined, the proposal narrative simply becomes a structured explanation of how the project will work and why it is needed.

Assessing Your Need

Before preparing a grant proposal, it is important to clearly understand the need your proposed project is intended to address. Grant funders want to see evidence that the program is responding to a real and documented problem within the community.

Key Question: *Do we have real data to support this need, or are we relying on assumptions?*

In many cases, organizations already have a general idea of the challenges they want to address. However, successful grant proposals require more than a general concern. They require clear evidence that demonstrates the scope and impact of the problem.

One of the most effective ways to assess need is by reviewing existing data and information already available within your organization or community. For local governments and public safety agencies, this may include:

- Crime statistics
- Emergency response data
- Fire incident reports
- Disaster risk assessments
- Demographic data
- Public health information
- Transportation or traffic safety data

These sources help demonstrate that the issue being addressed is supported by objective information rather than anecdotal observations.

Community engagement can also play an important role in identifying needs. Organizations may gather input through community meetings, stakeholder discussions, surveys, or collaboration with partner agencies. Input from community members, local organizations, and subject matter experts can help identify gaps in services and potential opportunities for new programs.

For example, a city may identify an increase in traffic related injuries through local police data. This information may support the development of a traffic safety education program funded through a transportation safety grant.

Similarly, a fire department may review incident data and identify an increase in residential fires within certain neighborhoods. This data could support a grant proposal for smoke alarm installation programs or community fire prevention education.

When developing a grant proposal, it is helpful to combine statistical data with real-world examples that illustrate how the problem affects individuals or communities. Data provides evidence of the scope of the issue, while real-world examples help demonstrate the human impact of the problem.

Strong need statements often include:

- Statistical data describing the issue
- Trends showing how the problem has changed over time
- Comparisons to regional or national averages
- Input from community stakeholders
- Examples illustrating the real-world impact of the problem

By clearly documenting the need for a proposed project, organizations can demonstrate to grant funders that the program addresses a legitimate issue and that funding the project will help produce meaningful improvements for the community.

Grant Writing Tip:

The strongest grant proposals clearly demonstrate the need for a project using both data and real-world examples. Reviewers should be able to understand the scope of the problem within the first few paragraphs of your proposal.

Evaluation Methods and Measurable Outcomes

When designing a grant-funded program, it is essential to demonstrate how the success of the program will be measured. Grant funders want to see clear evidence that the project will produce meaningful results and that those results can be evaluated using objective data.

Key Question: *How will we prove this project actually made a difference?*

Evaluation methods are the tools and processes used to determine whether a program is achieving its intended goals. These methods should be established during the planning phase of the project so that progress can be tracked from the beginning of the program through its completion.

In many cases, grant programs require applicants to describe both program outputs and program outcomes.

Program Outputs

Outputs refer to the direct activities or services provided through the program. Examples may include:

- Number of people served
- Number of training sessions conducted
- Number of pieces of equipment purchased

- Number of community outreach events held

Program Outcomes

Outcomes refer to the measurable changes that occur as a result of the program. These outcomes demonstrate the real impact of the project on the individuals or communities being served.

Examples of measurable outcomes may include:

- Reduction in crime rates
- Improved emergency response times
- Increased graduation rates for program participants
- Improved safety awareness among community members

For example, a nonprofit organization providing transitional housing for families experiencing homelessness might track the number of families served each year. However, the true measure of success would be how many of those families secure stable housing or employment after participating in the program.

Collecting accurate data is essential for demonstrating program success. Organizations should develop systems for tracking participation, services provided, and program outcomes throughout the life of the grant.

Example: Public Safety Grant Evaluation

Outputs

Train 150 community members in emergency preparedness.

Outcome

Within one year, 75% of participants report having a household emergency plan and emergency supply kit.

Common evaluation tools include:

- Participant surveys
- Program attendance records
- Performance data collected by the organization
- Follow up interviews with participants
- Statistical data from local agencies

Grant funders often require periodic program and financial reports throughout the duration of the grant. These reports allow funders to monitor progress and ensure that funds are being used as described in the proposal.

Because evaluation and reporting requirements can require significant staff time, organizations should plan ahead and ensure that someone is responsible for collecting data and maintaining accurate records.

In addition to demonstrating accountability, strong evaluation methods can help organizations improve their programs over time. By analyzing the data collected during a project, organizations can identify what worked well, what challenges were encountered, and how future programs can be strengthened.

Establishing clear evaluation methods and measurable outcomes not only improves the quality of a grant proposal, but also helps ensure that grant-funded programs produce lasting and meaningful results.

Research

Locating appropriate sources for grant funding is at least fifty percent of the grant process and often one of the most challenging parts. Many new grant writers assume the most difficult step is writing the proposal itself, but experienced grant writers know that identifying the right funding opportunity is just as important. A strong proposal submitted to the wrong grant program will almost certainly fail.

Key Question: *Are we targeting the right funding source, or just the most visible one?*

The first step in locating grant funding is identifying the government agency, corporation, or foundation most likely to support your project. Every grant program is created to address a specific need or priority. If your project does not clearly align with that priority, it will be difficult to receive funding regardless of how well the proposal is written.

It is also important to remember that the number of funding requests submitted to most grant programs far exceeds the available funding. This makes it critical to focus your efforts on opportunities where your program closely matches the goals of the funding agency.

One effective research strategy is to review previously funded projects. Many grant agencies publish lists of past award recipients on their websites. Reviewing these lists can help you determine whether your proposed program is similar to projects that have been funded in the past. If your project closely resembles previously funded programs, your chances of success may increase.

Grant Writing Tip:

Review previously funded projects whenever possible. If your proposed project closely resembles projects that have been funded in the past, your chances of success increase significantly.

Major Grant Programs for Public Safety Agencies

Public safety agencies such as fire departments, police departments, and emergency management offices often rely on grant funding to support equipment purchases, training programs, and community preparedness initiatives. While many grant opportunities exist, several major programs have historically provided significant funding for public safety agencies across the United States.

Understanding these programs can help agencies identify potential funding sources for critical projects.

Assistance to Firefighters Grant (AFG)

The Assistance to Firefighters Grant program, administered by the Federal Emergency Management Agency (FEMA), provides funding to fire departments and emergency medical services organizations.

AFG grants support:

- Firefighting equipment
- Personal protective equipment
- Training programs
- Emergency vehicles
- Wellness and fitness initiatives

Since its creation in 2001, the AFG program has provided billions of dollars in funding to improve the safety and operational capabilities of fire departments nationwide.

Staffing for Adequate Fire and Emergency Response (SAFER)

The SAFER grant program provides funding to fire departments to help increase the number of trained firefighters available to respond to emergencies.

SAFER grants are commonly used to:

- Hire additional firefighters
- Retain existing firefighters
- Support volunteer firefighter recruitment programs

These grants help departments maintain adequate staffing levels to protect their communities.

Emergency Management Performance Grant (EMPG)

The Emergency Management Performance Grant program supports state and local emergency management agencies in strengthening their preparedness and response capabilities.

EMPG funding is commonly used for:

- Emergency planning
- Training and exercises
- Emergency operations center improvements
- Disaster preparedness programs

These grants help communities develop the capacity to respond effectively to disasters and other emergencies.

Homeland Security Grant Program (HSGP)

The Homeland Security Grant Program provides funding to strengthen national preparedness and protect critical infrastructure.

This program includes several sub programs such as:

- State Homeland Security Program (SHSP)
- Urban Area Security Initiative (UASI)
- Operation Stonegarden

Funding may support equipment purchases, training, planning, and coordination between public safety agencies.

COPS Hiring Program

The Community Oriented Policing Services (COPS) Hiring Program provides funding to law enforcement agencies to hire additional officers and expand community policing efforts.

This program helps agencies strengthen relationships with the communities they serve while improving public safety.

Traffic Safety Grants

Traffic safety grants are often administered by state transportation agencies and support initiatives designed to reduce traffic accidents and fatalities.

Common traffic safety grant projects include:

- Impaired driving enforcement
- Traffic safety education campaigns

- Pedestrian and bicycle safety programs
- Law enforcement training

Why Public Safety Grants Matter

Grant funding plays a critical role in helping public safety agencies implement programs and purchase equipment that may not be possible through local budgets alone. By understanding available grant programs and developing strong proposals, agencies can secure funding that improves services and enhances the safety of their communities.

Federal Government Resources

For government agencies, the largest source of grant funding typically comes from federal and state programs. While private foundations and corporate grants can provide valuable support, government grants often provide the largest funding opportunities for public agencies and nonprofit organizations.

One of the most important resources for identifying federal grant opportunities is Grants.gov, the central portal used by the United States government to publish federal funding opportunities. Through this website, organizations can search for open funding announcements across dozens of federal agencies.

Most federal grant opportunities are now published as Notices of Funding Opportunity (NOFOs). These notices provide detailed information about eligibility requirements, application deadlines, funding amounts, and evaluation criteria.

Organizations applying for federal grants must also register in the System for Award Management (SAM.gov). Registration with SAM.gov provides organizations with a Unique Entity Identifier (UEI), which has replaced the older DUNS number previously required for federal grant applications. This registration process allows federal agencies to verify the identity of organizations receiving federal funds.

Because registration and verification can take several days to complete, it is recommended that organizations register well in advance of any grant application deadline.

Many federal agencies administer large grant programs. For example, the Federal Emergency Management Agency (FEMA) administers several major grant programs designed to strengthen emergency preparedness and public safety capabilities across the country. These programs support activities such as emergency response planning, equipment purchases, training, and disaster resilience.

State Agencies

State governments also administer many grant programs that support local governments, nonprofits, schools, and community organizations. State grants are often smaller than federal grants but can still provide significant funding for projects at the local level.

Many state agencies publish grant opportunities directly on their websites. In addition, many states maintain centralized grant portals where users can search for available funding opportunities by category or topic.

Examples of common state grant categories include:

- Public safety and emergency preparedness
- Workforce development
- Education programs
- Environmental protection

- Housing and community development
- Transportation and infrastructure

Because grant programs vary significantly from state to state, it is important to regularly review your state government's website for announcements and updates.

Local Sources

Although federal and state grants often provide the largest funding opportunities, local funding sources should not be overlooked. Local businesses, community foundations, and regional organizations sometimes offer grant programs designed to support projects within their communities.

These grants may not provide large amounts of funding, but they can be extremely valuable for pilot programs, community initiatives, or bridging funding gaps while larger grants are pursued.

Local funding opportunities may include:

- Community foundations
- Regional nonprofit organizations
- Corporate community giving programs
- Chambers of commerce
- Local philanthropic donors

Developing relationships within your community can also play an important role in identifying these opportunities.

Private and Corporate Foundation Resources

Private foundations and corporate giving programs provide another important source of grant funding. These organizations often support projects aligned with their mission, corporate values, or geographic priorities.

Several online tools can help organizations identify foundation funding opportunities. Some commonly used resources include:

- Foundation Directory Online
- Candid (formerly Foundation Center and GuideStar)
- Instrumentl
- GrantStation

Many public libraries provide free access to foundation research databases that would otherwise require a subscription.

As with government grants, it is important to review each foundation's funding priorities, geographic focus, and eligibility requirements before preparing a proposal.

Using Your Connections

In addition to formal grant programs, personal and professional connections can play an important role in identifying funding opportunities. Board members, donors, volunteers, and community leaders often have connections to foundations or corporate giving programs.

In some cases, a personal introduction to a foundation officer or corporate philanthropy manager can help bring attention to your project and open the door to future funding discussions.

Building strong relationships within your community and maintaining a positive reputation for your organization can greatly increase your chances of identifying funding opportunities that might otherwise go unnoticed.

Making Sure It's a Go

Before submitting a grant proposal, it is essential to confirm that your organization is fully prepared to implement the proposed project. One of the most common mistakes made by inexperienced grant writers is submitting a proposal without fully consulting the people who will actually carry out the program.

Key Question: *Is our organization truly ready to implement this project if it is funded?*

If your role is to identify funding opportunities and prepare grant proposals, you should work closely with the program staff who will be responsible for implementing the project. These individuals will ultimately be responsible for managing personnel, delivering services, collecting performance data, and preparing reports required by the grant funder.

Early collaboration ensures that everyone understands the scope of the project, the timeline, and the responsibilities involved. Without this coordination, it is easy to create unrealistic expectations or overlook operational challenges that may arise once the grant is awarded.

A good practice is to schedule a planning meeting with key staff before submitting a proposal. During this meeting you should discuss:

- The purpose of the project
- Staffing requirements
- Equipment or technology needs

- Program timeline
- Reporting and evaluation requirements
- Potential risks or implementation challenges

In many organizations, senior leadership approval is also required before submitting a grant application. This may include approval from an Executive Director, City Manager, Department Director, or governing board.

Securing internal approval early in the process ensures that the organization is fully committed to the project and prepared to meet the obligations that come with accepting grant funding.

Another important factor in modern grant applications is collaboration. Many grant programs now prioritize projects that demonstrate partnerships between multiple agencies or organizations. For example, a public safety grant proposal may involve collaboration between police departments, fire departments, schools, nonprofit organizations, or community groups.

Partnerships can strengthen a proposal by showing that the project will have a broader impact and that multiple stakeholders are committed to addressing the problem.

Grant Writing Tip:

Never submit a grant application without confirming that your organization is fully prepared to implement the project. Early coordination with program staff and leadership can prevent serious challenges after the award.

Matching Funds

Many grant programs require applicants to contribute matching funds toward the total cost of a project. Matching funds demonstrate that the applicant organization and its partners are invested in the success of the project.

Matching contributions can take several forms:

- Cash Match refers to funds contributed directly by the applicant organization or a partner organization. These funds are typically used to cover a portion of project costs such as personnel, equipment, or program expenses.

- In Kind Contributions refer to non-cash resources that support the project. Examples may include staff time, use of facilities, equipment, volunteer services, or donated materials. These contributions often have a documented value and can sometimes be counted toward the required match.

- Cost Sharing refer to matching requirements as cost sharing. This means that the total cost of the project is shared between the grant funder and the applicant organization.

For example, if a grant program requires a 25% match and the total project cost is $100,000, the grant funder may provide $75,000 while the applicant organization must contribute $25,000 through cash or eligible in-kind contributions.

It is important to carefully review grant guidelines to determine whether matching funds are required and what types of contributions are eligible.

Before submitting a proposal, you should confirm with your organization's finance staff that the required matching funds are available and properly documented. Failure to demonstrate the required match can result in a proposal being rejected during the review process.

> **Grant Writing Tip:**
>
> *Even when matching funds are not required, including a local contribution can strengthen your proposal by demonstrating commitment and increasing credibility with reviewers.*

In many cases, matching funds can also make a proposal more competitive even when they are not required. Demonstrating financial commitment and community support shows grant reviewers that the project has strong backing and a higher likelihood of success.

Letters of Support

Many grant programs encourage or require applicants to submit letters of support from partner organizations, community stakeholders, or public officials. These letters help demonstrate that the proposed project has broad support and that other organizations recognize the value of the project.

Letters of support can strengthen a proposal by showing that the applicant has established partnerships and that the project addresses a recognized community need. For public safety agencies, letters may come from neighboring jurisdictions, regional agencies, community organizations, or elected officials.

For example, a fire department applying for a grant to purchase new equipment may include letters from neighboring fire departments that participate in mutual aid agreements. These letters demonstrate that the equipment will benefit not only the applying agency, but also surrounding communities that rely on regional response cooperation.

Similarly, a police department seeking funding for traffic safety initiatives may obtain letters from hospitals, schools, or transportation agencies that support efforts to reduce traffic related injuries.

When requesting letters of support, it is helpful to provide the supporting organization with a brief description of the project and the purpose of the grant. This allows the letter to reinforce the goals of the proposal.

Letters of support are typically included as attachments to the grant application and should be signed by an authorized representative of the supporting organization.

While letters of support alone will not secure grant funding, they can strengthen a proposal by demonstrating collaboration and community support.

Grant Writing Tip:

Strong letters of support should reinforce your project, not repeat it. Provide your partners with key talking points so their letters highlight the importance and impact of the proposed program.

Benefit Cost Analysis (BCA)

Some grant programs require applicants to demonstrate that the benefits of a proposed project outweigh the costs of implementing it. This process is known as a Benefit Cost Analysis (BCA).

A BCA evaluates whether the long-term benefits of a project justify the investment of grant funds. The analysis compares the cost of implementing a project with the estimated financial or societal benefits that will result from the project.

Benefit Cost Analyses are most commonly used in disaster mitigation and infrastructure programs. For example, FEMA mitigation grants often require applicants to demonstrate that the cost of a project, such as flood protection or seismic retrofitting, is lower than the potential damage costs that could occur if the hazard event occurs.

In order for a project to qualify, the analysis must typically show that the benefit to cost ratio is greater than 1.0, meaning the expected benefits exceed the cost of the project.

Preparing a Benefit Cost Analysis can be technically complex and may require assistance from engineers, architects, economists, or other subject matter experts who can estimate damage scenarios and project costs.

For example, our city once explored pursuing a mitigation grant to retrofit the City Hall building for earthquake safety. The project had advanced far enough that our Letter of Intent was approved, allowing us to move forward with the application process.

However, when we worked with engineering and architectural consultants to complete the FEMA BCA calculations, the results showed that the projected benefits did not exceed the cost of the retrofit project. Because the required benefit to cost ratio could not be achieved, the project did not qualify under the program's funding criteria and we ultimately decided not to proceed with the application.

While this outcome was disappointing, it reinforced an important lesson: not every worthwhile project will qualify under a BCA driven grant program. These grants require a very specific alignment between project cost and projected hazard losses.

Although I have written many successful grant applications over the years, most of them did not require a formal Benefit Cost Analysis. However, for programs that do require it, applicants should carefully evaluate whether the project is likely to meet the required threshold before investing significant time and resources into the application process.

Understanding this requirement early can help organizations focus their efforts on projects that are more likely to meet the funding criteria. Grant writing often involves exploring opportunities that may or may not ultimately qualify for funding. Even when a project does not move forward, the process can still provide valuable insight into future funding opportunities.

Writing A Proposal: A Step-by-Step Guide

Once you have identified a grant opportunity that aligns with your project and confirmed that your organization is prepared to implement the program, the next step is preparing the grant proposal.

Key Question: *Can we clearly and confidently tell the story of our project from start to finish?*

Many people assume that writing a grant proposal is the most difficult part of the process. In reality, most grant proposals follow a structured format and include specific questions that must be answered by the applicant. If you have completed the planning steps described earlier in this guide, much of the information needed for your proposal should already be available.

Most grant applications require similar sections, although the exact format may vary depending on the funding agency. Federal, state, and foundation grants typically request information in the following areas:

- Cover Letter
- Executive Summary
- Problem Statement or Statement of Need
- Project Narrative or Program Description

- Organizational Overview
- Project Goals and Objectives
- Project Timeline
- Evaluation Plan
- Budget and Budget Justification
- Key Staff and Organizational Capacity
- Required Attachments

Many grant programs now require proposals to be submitted through online grant management systems. These systems often provide specific text boxes for each section of the proposal and may include character limits. Because of this, it is helpful to draft your responses in advance before entering them into the online system.

Although each grant program has its own specific requirements, the sections described below represent the most common elements of a competitive grant proposal.

Cover Letter

The cover letter provides a brief introduction to your organization and your funding request. It should clearly state the amount of funding being requested and summarize the purpose of the project.

For example:

"Organization X respectfully requests funding in the amount of $150,000 to support the implementation of a community emergency preparedness program designed to strengthen disaster readiness among residents of City X."

The cover letter should be brief and professional and should reinforce how the proposed project aligns with the mission of the funding agency.

In government agencies, the cover letter is often signed by an authorized official such as the City Manager, Department Director, or Executive Director.

Executive Summary

The executive summary provides a concise overview of the proposed project. In many cases, this section is written last, even though it appears at the beginning of the proposal.

The executive summary should briefly describe:

- The problem being addressed
- The proposed solution
- The population or community being served
- The amount of funding requested
- The expected outcomes of the project

Because some reviewers may read the executive summary first, this section should clearly communicate the purpose and importance of the project.

Problem Statement

The problem statement describes the issue that the proposed project is designed to address. A strong problem statement combines data, research, and real-world examples to demonstrate why the project is necessary.

For public safety agencies, this section may include information such as:

- Crime statistics
- Emergency response data
- Population growth trends
- Hazard risk assessments
- Community vulnerability data

The goal is to clearly demonstrate that a real problem exists and that addressing this issue will improve safety, services, or quality of life within the community.

Project Narrative

The project narrative is often the most important section of the grant proposal. This is where the applicant describes how the proposed project will operate and how it will address the problem described earlier.

A strong project narrative should answer the following questions:

- Who will implement the project?
- What activities will take place?
- Where the program will operate?
- When the project will occur?
- Why the program is needed?

- How the project will achieve its goals?

The narrative should be clear, organized, and focused on explaining how the project will produce measurable results.

Organizational Overview

The organizational overview provides background information about the agency or organization submitting the proposal. This section should demonstrate that the organization has the experience, leadership, and infrastructure necessary to successfully manage the proposed project.

Information that may be included in this section includes:

- Organizational mission and history
- Population served
- Staffing structure
- Past program successes
- Experience managing grant-funded programs

For government agencies, this section may also include information about the jurisdiction served, population size, and the department responsible for implementing the project.

Project Goals and Objectives

Goals describe the overall purpose of the project, while objectives describe the specific actions that will be taken to achieve those goals.

Goals are generally broad statements describing the desired outcome of the program.

Objectives should be specific, measurable, and time based. A common framework used in grant writing is the SMART model, meaning objectives should be:

- Specific
- Measurable
- Achievable
- Relevant
- Time bound

Clearly defined objectives help grant reviewers understand how the project will be implemented and how success will be measured.

Project Timeline

The project timeline provides an overview of the major milestones associated with the project. This section shows the grant funder when specific activities will occur and how the project will progress from start to completion.

Typical timeline milestones may include:

- Project startup
- Equipment procurement
- Hiring or training staff
- Program implementation
- Community outreach activities
- Evaluation and reporting

Providing a clear timeline demonstrates that the project has been thoughtfully planned and that the organization is prepared to implement it effectively.

Evaluation Plan

The evaluation plan describes how the success of the project will be measured. This section should align closely with the goals and objectives described earlier.

Evaluation methods may include:

- Performance metrics
- Statistical analysis
- Participant surveys
- Program outcome tracking
- Independent program evaluation

Grant funders want to see evidence that the project will produce measurable results and that the organization will track those results throughout the life of the grant.

Budget and Budget Justification

The budget provides a detailed breakdown of the costs associated with implementing the project. Grant funders often provide a specific budget template that applicants must complete.

Common budget categories include:

- Personnel costs
- Equipment

- Training
- Travel
- Supplies
- Contractual services

The budget justification explains how each cost supports the project and why the expense is necessary. It is important that the budget and the project narrative align and that all calculations are accurate.

Key Staff

This section highlights the qualifications and experience of the individuals responsible for managing and implementing the project.

Grant reviewers want to know that the project will be managed by individuals with the appropriate skills and experience. Short biographies or summaries of key staff members are often included, and some grant programs may require resumes as attachments.

The Municipal Grant Lifecycle

The grant application is only one part of a larger process. The following lifecycle illustrates how grant-funded projects move from community need to long-term impact.

Figure 1: Municipal Grant Lifecycle

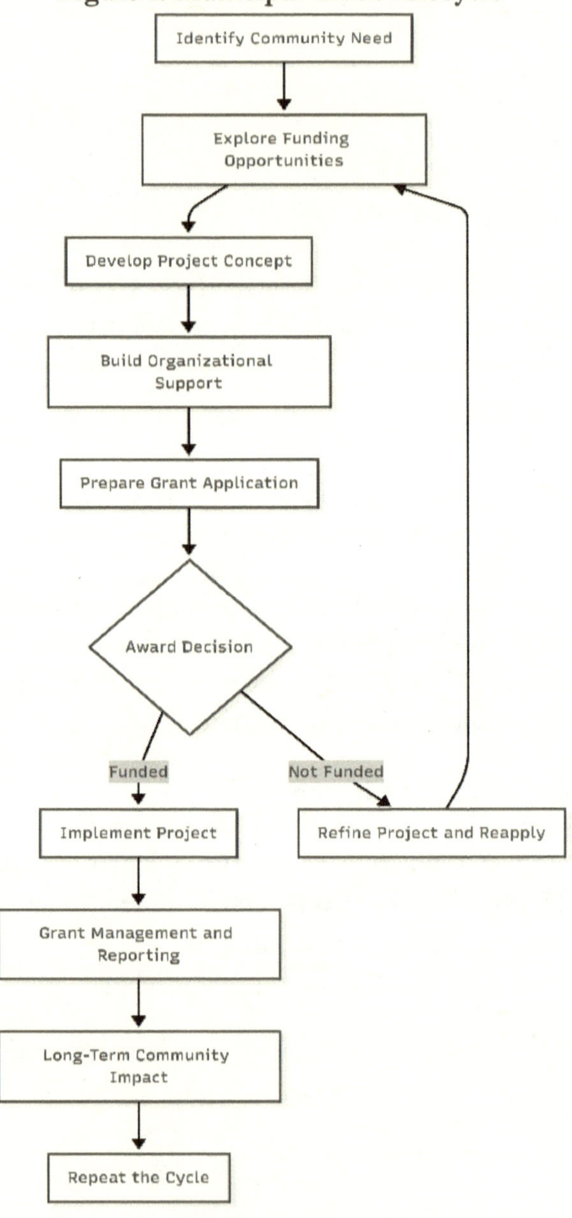

Successful grant programs repeat this cycle over time.

Using Artificial Intelligence in Grant Writing

Artificial intelligence tools such as ChatGPT are increasingly being used to assist with writing tasks, including grant applications. While these tools can be helpful, they should be used carefully and as a supplement to, not a replacement for, the grant writing process.

Some individuals may assume that grant questions can simply be entered into an AI tool to generate a complete and competitive response. In practice, successful grant applications require a clear understanding of the organization, the project, and the specific requirements of the funding agency.

AI tools can assist with certain aspects of grant writing, including:

- Organizing ideas into a structured format
- Improving clarity and readability
- Generating draft language based on provided information
- Summarizing background information or research
- Refining grammar and sentence structure

However, AI tools do not have direct knowledge of your organization, your community, or the specific needs your project is intended to address. As a result, responses generated without proper input may be too general, lack supporting detail, or fail to align with the priorities of the funding agency.

To use AI effectively in grant writing, consider the following approach:

Start with Your Own Content

Develop your project concept, identify your needs, and gather key data before using AI tools. The strongest grant applications are based on real information and clearly defined objectives.

Use AI to Refine, Not Replace

AI can help improve wording and organization, but it should not replace the development of the proposal itself. Always review and edit AI generated content to ensure accuracy and relevance.

Align With Grant Requirements

Each funding opportunity has specific criteria and priorities. Ensure that any content generated aligns directly with the grant guidelines and evaluation criteria.

Verify All Information

Do not rely on AI to generate factual data or statistics without verification. All information included in a grant proposal should be accurate and supported by reliable sources.

Maintain Your Voice and Expertise

Grant reviewers are evaluating your organization's understanding of the problem and its ability to deliver results. Your experience and knowledge should remain central to the proposal.

AI tools can be a useful addition to the grant writing process when used appropriately. However, successful grant applications still depend on thoughtful planning, accurate information, and a clear understanding of the community needs being addressed.

Grant Writing Tip:

Artificial intelligence can improve clarity and organization, but it cannot replace real project knowledge. The strongest grant proposals are built on accurate data, clear objectives, and a deep understanding of the community being served.

Example: Using AI to Strengthen a Grant Response

Artificial intelligence tools can be most effective when used to refine and strengthen content that has already been developed. Below is a simple example of how AI can be used to improve a grant response.

Step 1: Start with Your Own Content

Initial Draft (Prepared by Staff)

Our department needs new communication equipment because the current radios are outdated and do not always work properly during emergency incidents. This creates safety concerns for both personnel and the public.

Step 2: Provide Context to the AI Tool

Instead of asking AI to write the entire response, provide specific details:

Prompt Example:

"Improve the clarity and professionalism of the following grant statement. This is for a fire department requesting funding for updated radio communications. Emphasize firefighter safety, reliability during emergency incidents, and the impact on response coordination."

Step 3: AI-Refined Response

Revised Draft

The department is seeking funding to replace outdated communication equipment that has become increasingly unreliable during emergency operations. Reliable communication is essential for effective incident command, coordination among responding units, and the safety of both personnel and the public.

Upgrading radio systems will improve operational efficiency, enhance situational awareness, and ensure that critical information is communicated clearly during emergency incidents.

Step 4: Final Review and Customization

The revised response should then be reviewed and adjusted to include:

- Specific examples from the department
- Data or incident history
- Alignment with the grant's evaluation criteria

Key Takeaway

AI tools are most effective when used to enhance well-developed content, not replace it. Strong grant proposals begin with accurate information, clear objectives, and a solid understanding of the project being proposed. In contrast, submitting AI-generated responses without customization often results in generic proposals that are less competitive and may not fully address the requirements of the funding agency.

Grant Writing AI Prompt Template

The following template can be used to help generate or refine grant proposal content using artificial intelligence tools. This template is most effective when you provide detailed and accurate information about your organization and project.

Basic Prompt Template

"Act as a professional grant writer. Improve and refine the following draft response for a grant application.

Organization Type: [Fire Department / Police Department / City Government / Nonprofit]

Project Description: [Brief description of what you are requesting funding for]

Community Need: [Describe the problem or need being addressed]

Key Outcomes: [What results will this project achieve]

Funding Purpose: [What the grant funds will be used for]

Additional Context: [Any relevant details such as population served, call volume, or existing challenges]

Please ensure the response is clear, professional, and aligned with typical grant evaluation criteria such as need, impact, and feasibility."

Example Use

Input:

Organization Type: Fire Department

Project Description: Replacement of outdated portable radios

Community Need: Radios frequently fail during emergency incidents

Key Outcomes: Improved communication and firefighter safety

Funding Purpose: Purchase of new portable and mobile radios

Additional Context: Department responds to over 8,000 calls annually

AI Output (Example)

The department is seeking funding to replace outdated portable radio equipment that has become unreliable during emergency operations. Reliable communication is critical to ensuring effective coordination among responding units, maintaining situational awareness, and protecting the safety of both firefighters and the public.

With an annual call volume exceeding 8,000 incidents, the need for dependable communication systems is essential. Upgrading radio equipment will enhance operational efficiency, improve response coordination, and support safer and more effective emergency operations.

Important Notes

AI-generated content should always be reviewed and customized to reflect your organization's actual data, project details, and the specific requirements of the funding opportunity.

The most competitive grant applications are those that combine clear, locally relevant information with well-structured and professionally written responses.

Grant Writing Tip:

The quality of AI-generated content depends on the quality of the information provided. Vague inputs will result in vague responses.

Evaluating Yourself

Before submitting a grant proposal, it is critical to carefully review the entire application to ensure that all requirements have been met. Many grant proposals are rejected during the initial review stage simply because the applicant failed to follow instructions or omitted required information.

Key Question: *If I were the reviewer, would I fund this proposal?*

Grant funders often receive hundreds of applications for a single funding opportunity. Because of this, reviewers frequently conduct an initial screening process to ensure that proposals meet all eligibility and submission requirements. Applications that do not follow the instructions outlined in the funding announcement may be considered non responsive and removed from further review.

For this reason, the first rule of grant writing is simple:

- Follow the instructions.

Grant guidelines often specify formatting requirements, page limits, required attachments, and submission procedures. These instructions should be reviewed carefully before beginning the proposal and again prior to submission.

Most grant programs now require proposals to be submitted through an online application portal. These systems often prevent incomplete applications from being submitted, but it is still the responsibility of the applicant to ensure that all required sections are complete and accurate.

Once a draft proposal has been completed, it is helpful to have several individuals review the document before submission. Each reviewer can provide a different perspective and help identify potential issues.

Recommended reviewers may include:

- Program staff responsible for implementing the project

- Finance staff responsible for the budget

- Supervisors or department leadership
- A colleague unfamiliar with the project who can provide an objective review of the proposal.

Finance staff should carefully review the budget to ensure that all costs are accurate and that any required matching funds are properly documented.

A colleague unfamiliar with the project can provide valuable feedback by identifying sections that may be unclear or confusing. If someone outside the project team cannot easily understand the proposal, reviewers may experience the same difficulty.

In addition to reviewing the technical requirements of the proposal, applicants should also consider the overall tone and clarity of the narrative. Effective proposals present a clear solution to a defined problem and communicate confidence in the organization's ability to implement the project.

Before submitting the proposal, ask yourself the following questions:

- Does the proposal clearly describe the problem being addressed?
- Does the project provide a realistic solution to that problem?
- Are the goals and objectives measurable?
- Does the budget align with the proposed activities?
- Have all required attachments been included?

Careful review before submission can significantly improve the quality of a grant proposal and reduce the risk of errors that could affect the application's competitiveness.

Grant Writing Tip:

If someone unfamiliar with your project cannot easily understand your proposal, reviewers may have the same difficulty. Always have an outside reader review your application before submission.

Grant Proposal Checklist

Many successful grant applications are the result of careful preparation and review. This checklist can help ensure that important elements of the proposal are completed before submission. Before submitting a grant application, review the following checklist to ensure that all required elements of the proposal have been completed.

Project Development

☐ A clear community need or problem has been identified

☐ Data or documentation supports the need for the project

☐ The proposed project directly addresses the identified need

☐ Project goals and objectives are clearly defined

☐ Expected outcomes are measurable and realistic

Organizational Readiness

☐ The organization has the staff and resources to implement the project

☐ Leadership supports the proposed project

☐ Partner organizations have been identified if needed

☐ Letters of support have been obtained where appropriate

Budget Preparation

☐ The project budget reflects the activities described in the proposal

☐ Budget calculations are accurate and clearly explained

☐ Required matching funds have been identified

☐ The finance department has reviewed the budget if applicable

Proposal Narrative

☐ The proposal clearly describes the problem being addressed

☐ The project activities are explained in a logical sequence

☐ The narrative demonstrates how the project will benefit the community

☐ The proposal aligns with the priorities of the funding agency

Supporting Documentation

☐ All required attachments have been included

☐ Letters of support are signed and dated

☐ Required certifications and assurances are completed

☐ Any required Benefit Cost Analysis or technical documentation is included

Final Review

☐ The proposal has been proofread for clarity and accuracy

☐ Page limits and formatting requirements have been followed

☐ All required signatures have been obtained

☐ The application has been reviewed by at least one additional person

Submission

☐ The proposal has been uploaded or submitted according to the funding agency's instructions

☐ A copy of the final application has been saved for organizational records

Grant Writing Tip:

Save a copy of every grant application you submit. Successful proposals often serve as templates for future funding opportunities.

After the Fact

Once a grant proposal has been submitted, the waiting process begins. Funding decisions may take several weeks or even months depending on the complexity of the grant program and the number of applications received.

Regardless of the outcome, it is important to maintain organized records of all grant proposals submitted. Keeping copies of the proposal, the funding announcement, and supporting documentation can be extremely helpful for future grant opportunities.

Grant Writing Tip:

A grant is not truly successful until it is properly managed and closed out. Strong post-award management builds credibility and improves your chances of future funding.

Congratulations, you have funding!

If your proposal is selected for funding, the first step is to acknowledge the award and express appreciation to the grant funder. A brief letter or email thanking the funding agency for their support helps establish a positive relationship and demonstrates professionalism.

In many government agencies and nonprofit organizations, acceptance of a grant award must be approved by the organization's governing body. This may include a City Council, Board of Supervisors, or Board of Directors. The governing body typically approves the grant through a formal resolution authorizing the organization to accept the funding and implement the project.

Once the grant is accepted, the project moves into the implementation phase. This stage often includes activities such as:

- Establishing project accounts and budgets
- Purchasing equipment or services
- Hiring or assigning project staff
- Launching program activities

- Tracking performance metrics

Follow-Up Reports and Accountability

Receiving grant funding also creates a responsibility to demonstrate that the funds are being used appropriately and that the project is achieving its intended outcomes.

Most grant programs require periodic reports throughout the life of the project. These reports may include:

- Program progress reports
- Financial expenditure reports
- Performance metrics
- Documentation of project activities

Grant funders may also conduct site visits or request additional documentation to verify that project activities are being carried out as described in the proposal.

Maintaining accurate records throughout the project is essential for successful grant management. This includes documentation of financial transactions, project activities, and performance outcomes.

Organizations that manage grant funds responsibly and submit reports on time build strong relationships with funding agencies, which can improve the chances of receiving future grant awards.

You Didn't Receive the Grant

Not every grant proposal will be successful. In fact, many competitive grant programs fund only a small percentage of applicants. If your proposal is not selected, consider contacting the grant funder to request feedback if it is available. Reviewer comments can provide valuable insight into how your proposal might be improved for future funding opportunities.

In some cases, unsuccessful proposals can be revised and resubmitted during the next funding cycle.

Grant writing is often an iterative process. Each proposal provides an opportunity to improve your approach, strengthen your program design, and refine your narrative.

Organizations that remain persistent and continue refining their proposals often achieve success over time.

When Hiring a Grant Writer Makes Sense

Many organizations consider hiring a grant writer when they are pursuing external funding. While this guide is designed to help organizations develop their own grant writing skills, there are situations where working with an experienced grant writer can be beneficial.

For organizations that lack internal staff with grant writing experience, hiring a professional grant writer may help identify funding opportunities, develop stronger proposals, and navigate complex application requirements.

Grant writers can also be valuable when an organization is pursuing a large or highly competitive funding opportunity that requires significant technical writing, research, and coordination among multiple partners.

However, organizations should remember that even when a grant writer is hired, the success of the proposal still depends on the information and collaboration provided by the organization itself. A grant writer cannot replace the expertise of the program staff who will ultimately implement the project.

If your organization decides to hire a grant writer, there are several factors you should consider.

Experience is one of the most important qualifications. Ask the grant writer about the types of grants they have written and the agencies or organizations they have worked with. Experienced grant writers should be able to provide examples of successful proposals or describe the types of funding programs they have helped secure.

It is also helpful to ask for references from other organizations that have worked with the grant writer. This can provide insight into their professionalism, reliability, and ability to meet deadlines.

Another important consideration is how the grant writer is compensated. Some grant writers work on an hourly basis or for a flat project fee. Others may offer services such as grant research, proposal development, or grant management support.

Organizations should be cautious about grant writers who request payment based solely on a percentage of the grant award. In many cases, this type of compensation structure is discouraged or prohibited by professional grant writing organizations and funding agencies.

Even when working with a grant writer, the organization should remain actively involved in the proposal development process. Program staff and leadership must review the proposal carefully, confirm that all information is accurate, and ensure that the proposed project is realistic and achievable.

Ultimately, whether you choose to write grants internally or work with a professional grant writer, the most important factor is ensuring that your organization has a clear program concept, strong supporting data, and the capacity to successfully implement the proposed project. In many local government agencies, grant writing responsibilities are handled internally by analysts, emergency managers, or program staff who are familiar with the community's needs and operational priorities.

Ethics

Ethics play an important role in grant writing and grant management. Organizations receiving grant funding are entrusted with public or philanthropic resources that must be used responsibly and in accordance with the terms of the grant agreement.

Grant proposals should always present accurate and truthful information. Applicants should avoid exaggerating needs, inflating statistics, or misrepresenting the organization's capabilities in order to increase the chances of receiving funding. Misleading information can damage the organization's credibility and may lead to the loss of future funding opportunities.

Transparency is also essential when managing grant funds. Organizations must ensure that grant funds are used only for the purposes described in the approved proposal and budget. Financial records should be carefully maintained and made available for review if requested by the grant funder.

Grant writers should also avoid conflicts of interest. Individuals involved in the grant process should disclose any relationships that may influence funding decisions or project implementation.

Maintaining strong ethical standards helps build trust with funding agencies and strengthens the organization's reputation within the grant making community.

Conclusion

Grant writing may appear complex at first, but it is ultimately a structured and learnable process. Organizations that take the time to clearly identify community needs, develop realistic programs, and carefully follow grant guidelines often find that external funding can significantly strengthen their services.

Throughout this guide, we have explored the key steps involved in the grant process, from identifying funding opportunities and assessing organizational readiness to preparing competitive proposals and managing grants responsibly after they are awarded.

While every grant program has unique requirements, the fundamental principles remain the same: understand the need, develop a clear solution, and communicate that solution effectively to the funding agency.

For organizations willing to invest the time to research opportunities, build partnerships, and prepare thoughtful proposals, grant funding can become an important tool for improving public safety, expanding services, and strengthening communities.

PART III: PRACTICAL TOOLS

Grant Readiness Self-Assessment

Before investing time in preparing a grant application, organizations should determine whether they are ready to pursue grant funding. Successful grants require more than a good idea. They require organizational capacity, leadership support, and the ability to manage the project after funding is awarded.

Key Question: *Are we truly ready to pursue grant funding, or just interested in the idea of it?*

Use the following checklist to evaluate whether your organization is prepared to pursue grant opportunities.

Organizational Readiness

☐ Our organization has clearly identified a problem or need that requires funding.

☐ We have data or documentation that supports the need for the proposed project.

☐ Our leadership supports pursuing grant funding.

☐ We have staff available to assist with developing the grant proposal.

☐ Our organization has experience managing projects or programs similar to the proposed grant project.

Financial Readiness

☐ Our organization has financial systems capable of tracking grant expenditures.

☐ We understand whether the grant requires matching funds.

☐ We have identified potential funding sources for required matching funds.

☐ Our finance staff is able to assist with budget preparation and financial reporting.

☐ We understand that some grants operate on a reimbursement basis.

Program Readiness

☐ We have a clear description of the project we want to implement.

☐ We know who will manage the project if funding is awarded.

☐ We have identified measurable outcomes for the project.

☐ We understand the timeline for implementing the program.

☐ We have identified any partners or stakeholders that should be involved.

Grant Management Readiness

☐ We understand that grant management requires ongoing reporting and documentation.

☐ We are prepared to track program performance and financial expenditures.

☐ We have staff available to manage grant reporting requirements.

☐ We understand that receiving a grant often requires significant administrative work after the award.

Final Evaluation

If your organization answered "Yes" to most of these questions, you are likely well prepared to pursue grant funding.

If several questions were answered "No," you may want to address those issues before investing time in developing a grant proposal.

Preparing your organization in advance can greatly increase the chances of securing and successfully managing grant funding.

Top 10 Grant Writing Tips (Quick Reference)

This section provides a quick reference to key grant writing tips discussed throughout this guide. Each of these concepts is explained in greater detail within the relevant sections of the book.

1. Start with a clear problem statement. Grant reviewers must understand the issue you are addressing before they can appreciate your proposed solution.

2. Make sure the grant opportunity matches your project. Do not apply for funding simply because it is available. Ensure that your project aligns with the goals of the funding program.

3. Follow the instructions carefully. Failure to follow formatting or submission requirements can result in automatic disqualification.

4. Use data to support your proposal. Statistics, research, and community data strengthen the credibility of your request.

5. Develop measurable objectives. Grant funders want to see clear evidence that your project will produce meaningful results.

6. Create a realistic budget. Ensure that the budget aligns with the activities described in your proposal.

7. Collaborate with stakeholders. Partnerships with other organizations can strengthen your proposal and support.

8. Proofread your proposal carefully. Spelling and grammatical errors can undermine the professionalism of your application.

9. Plan for reporting and evaluation. Demonstrating how you will measure success is an essential part of a competitive proposal.

10. Do not be discouraged by rejection. Many successful grants are awarded only after proposals have been revised and resubmitted.

Final Checklist for Submitting Your Proposal

Before submitting your grant proposal, confirm the following:

☐ The proposal meets all eligibility requirements

☐ The narrative clearly explains the problem and proposed solution

☐ Goals and objectives are measurable

☐ The budget is accurate and consistent with the narrative

☐ Required attachments are included

☐ The proposal has been reviewed by program staff and finance staff

☐ All required signatures have been obtained

☐ The application has been submitted before the deadline

Taking the time to complete this final review can help ensure that your proposal is competitive and ready for evaluation.

Additional Resources

There are many resources available to assist organizations in identifying funding opportunities and improving their grant writing skills.

Common resources include:

Federal Grant Resources

Grants.gov

SAM.gov

Foundation Research Tools

Candid (formerly Foundation Center and GuideStar)

Foundation Directory Online

Instrumentl

GrantStation

Professional Organizations

Grant Professionals Association

National Grants Management Association

Local Resources

Public libraries

Community foundations

University research centers

These resources can help organizations stay informed about new funding opportunities and develop stronger grant proposals.

Establishing a Municipal Grant Process

As local governments pursue more grant opportunities, it becomes increasingly important to establish a structured process for identifying, reviewing, and managing grant applications. Without a clear process, departments may pursue funding opportunities that do not align with organizational priorities or create long-term financial obligations for the city.

Many municipalities develop internal procedures to ensure that grant opportunities are reviewed carefully before an application is submitted.

These processes often include several key components.

Identifying Grant Opportunities

Grant opportunities may be identified by city staff, grant coordinators, consultants, or individual departments. Once identified, the opportunity is typically shared with department leadership to determine whether the funding aligns with the goals of the organization.

In many cases, departments are encouraged to monitor professional publications, newsletters, and other sources for potential funding opportunities that may support their programs.

Request to Apply for Grant

Before preparing a full application, many cities require departments to submit a brief request to apply for grant funding. This request provides an overview of the project and allows leadership to evaluate the opportunity before significant staff time is invested.

Typical information requested in this type of form may include:

- Grant program name

- Project description
- Total funding requested
- Grant deadline
- Matching fund requirements
- Staffing or operational impacts

For example, a Request to Apply for Grants form may summarize the project, identify the department responsible for administering the grant, and outline any financial commitments required by the city.

This step helps ensure that leadership is aware of potential funding opportunities and can evaluate whether the project aligns with organizational priorities.

Administrative Review

Once the request is submitted, the proposed project is often reviewed by executive leadership. This review helps determine whether the city should proceed with the application.

Depending on the scope of the project, the request may be approved administratively, referred to the City Council for consideration, or denied if the project is not consistent with the city's priorities.

A structured review process helps prevent situations where departments pursue grants that may require long-term funding commitments or create operational challenges.

Grant Application and Tracking

If approval is granted, the department may proceed with preparing the grant application. Many cities maintain a centralized tracking system to monitor grant applications from submission through award and project completion.

Tracking systems may include information such as:

- Grant program name
- Project description
- Funding amount requested
- Application status
- Award decisions

Maintaining a centralized tracking system allows city leadership to monitor grant activity and maintain awareness of projects that may affect future budgets or staffing.

A structured grant process also helps ensure that departments communicate with leadership and coordinate with other city divisions when pursuing funding opportunities.

Smaller agencies may not have formal grant procedures, but establishing even a simple internal review process can help ensure that funding opportunities are pursued strategically.

Building a Grant Culture in Local Government

Over time, I began to notice that organizations tend to approach grant funding in different ways. Some pursue grants only occasionally, while others develop a culture that actively seeks funding opportunities to improve services. In my experience, most organizations move through several stages as they become more effective at securing grants.

The Four Levels of Municipal Grant Maturity

Level 1 – Reactive Grant Seeking

At this stage, agencies apply for grants only when someone happens to notice a funding opportunity.

Characteristics:

- No dedicated grant writer
- Opportunities are discovered randomly
- Applications are rushed near deadlines
- Departments work independently

Example scenario:

A department hears about a grant shortly before the deadline and tries to submit something quickly.

Many smaller agencies operate at this level.

Level 2 – Organized Grant Pursuit

At this stage, the organization begins paying attention to grant opportunities and becomes more organized in its efforts.

Characteristics:

- Someone is responsible for monitoring grant opportunities
- Departments occasionally collaborate
- Applications become more competitive

- Leadership begins to recognize the value of grants

Many cities begin to see their first major grant successes at this stage.

Level 3 – Strategic Grant Development

At this level, the organization begins aligning grant opportunities with long-term operational goals.

Characteristics:

- Departments coordinate on funding priorities
- Projects are planned in advance of grant cycles
- Supporting data and documentation are prepared early
- Leadership supports grant development

The organization is no longer reacting. It is strategically pursuing funding.

Level 4 – Institutional Grant Culture

This is the highest level of maturity and relatively few cities reach it.

At this stage, grant funding becomes part of the organization's long-term improvement strategy.

Characteristics:

- Multiple departments pursue grants
- Staff understand the grant process
- Leadership supports grant management

- Projects build on previous successes

Over time, these improvements accumulate and begin transforming the organization.

My fire department's progression from ISO Class 4 to ISO Class 1 is a perfect example of this type of long-term impact. Equipment upgrades, staffing improvements, communications systems, and training programs all contribute to stronger fire protection capabilities.

Final Thoughts: Grant Writing as a Leadership Tool

Throughout my career in municipal government, I have had the opportunity to work on a wide range of grant-funded projects supporting fire protection, law enforcement, infrastructure, and emergency management programs. While each grant had its own requirements and challenges, they all shared one common theme: they helped strengthen the ability of our community to respond to emergencies and protect the public.

Key Question: *How can grant writing be used to strengthen our organization over time?*

Many people view grant writing as a technical process focused primarily on completing applications and meeting funding requirements. While those tasks are certainly important, successful grant writing involves much more than simply filling out forms.

Grant writing is often about identifying opportunities, building relationships, and helping organizations improve their capabilities over time. In many cases, the most valuable grant opportunities arise from conversations with colleagues, collaboration between departments, and a willingness to explore new ideas.

Some of the projects described in this book began with simple questions:

- Could this program help our department?
- Is there a funding opportunity that might address this problem?
- Who else within the organization might benefit from this grant?

By asking these questions and working with others across the organization, it is often possible to identify opportunities that might otherwise go unnoticed.

Another important lesson from these experiences is that the work does not end when a grant is awarded. Managing grant funding requires accountability, documentation, and consistent communication with funding agencies. Organizations that approach grant management with the same level of professionalism used in preparing the application are more likely to build strong relationships with grant providers and remain competitive for future funding opportunities.

Over time, the cumulative impact of these efforts can be significant. Equipment upgrades, improved staffing levels, training programs, and enhanced emergency coordination capabilities all contribute to stronger public safety services for the community.

For those interested in pursuing grant funding, the most important advice is simple: be persistent, remain curious, and look for opportunities to help your organization improve. Successful grant writing is rarely the result of a single application. It is the product of ongoing effort, collaboration, and a commitment to strengthening the services provided to the community.

Continuing Your Grant Writing Journey

Grant writing is a skill that develops with practice and experience. While the process may seem complex at first, each proposal you prepare provides an opportunity to refine your approach, strengthen your writing, and better understand how funding programs operate.

Many successful grant writers began exactly where you may be today, preparing their first applications, learning the requirements of funding agencies, and gradually building confidence through experience. Over time, grant writing becomes less about filling out forms and more about clearly communicating the needs of a community and the value of a proposed solution.

One of the most effective ways to improve as a grant writer is to stay engaged with professional networks and funding organizations. Many federal and state agencies offer informational webinars, workshops, and guidance materials that can help applicants better understand program priorities and evaluation criteria.

It is also helpful to review previously funded projects whenever possible. These examples often provide insight into the types of proposals that funding agencies consider strong and competitive.

Equally important is maintaining strong relationships within your own organization. Successful grant projects often involve collaboration between departments, leadership support, and coordination with financial and administrative staff.

Over time, organizations that actively pursue grant opportunities often develop a culture that recognizes the value of external funding as a tool to strengthen programs, improve services, and enhance community safety.

Whether you are seeking funding for equipment, staffing, infrastructure improvements, or community programs, grant writing provides a pathway to bring new resources into your organization and expand what is possible.

With preparation, persistence, and a commitment to learning, grant writing can become one of the most valuable tools available to support the work of public service organizations.

About the Author

Walter Amedee holds a Master's Degree in Public Administration with an emphasis in Criminal Justice Administration and has more than 27 years of experience in municipal government and public safety. He currently serves as an Emergency Manager and has spent much of his career supporting public safety operations and community preparedness initiatives.

Throughout his career, he has successfully written and managed more than one hundred grant applications securing over $5 million in funding for fire, police, public works, and emergency preparedness programs. These grants have supported equipment purchases, training initiatives, emergency preparedness programs, and infrastructure improvements that strengthen community safety and resilience.

His experience includes federal, state, and local grant programs supporting public safety, disaster preparedness, and community development. Through his work in local government, he has helped agencies identify funding opportunities and develop programs that improve services and enhance the safety of the communities they serve.

For workshops, consulting, or bulk agency book orders, visit www.walteramedee.com.

Bring These Strategies to Your Organization

Based on the strategies outlined in this book and more than $6.7 million in successfully secured funding, your organization can strengthen its ability to compete for and win grant funding.

Whether you are just getting started or looking to improve your success rate, guidance and real-world experience can make a difference.

Request a Workshop or Training

Workshops and training sessions are available for:

- Fire Departments
- Law Enforcement Agencies
- Emergency Management Programs
- Local Government Staff
- Nonprofit Organizations

Each session is designed to provide practical, real-world strategies that can be applied immediately within your organization.

Take the Next Step

Scan the QR code below to request a workshop or schedule a training:

Or visit: www.walteramedee.com

Bulk book orders and agency training packages are also available.

Acknowledgments

This book reflects many years of experience working in municipal government and public safety, and it would not have been possible without the collaboration and support of many individuals along the way.

I would like to thank the leadership and staff of the City of National City for their continued commitment to public service and their willingness to pursue opportunities that strengthen the community. The projects described in this book are the result of coordinated efforts across departments, including fire, police, public works, finance, and administration.

I am also grateful to the many colleagues, partners, and organizations who contributed their time and expertise to the success of these grant-funded projects. Their dedication to improving public safety and municipal services made these efforts possible.

Finally, I would like to thank my wife for her unwavering support throughout my career, and my daughter, who inspired this book before she was even born.

www.ingramcontent.com/pod-product-compliance
Lightning Source LLC
LaVergne TN
LVHW090531110826
845146LV00003B/1058

* 9 7 9 8 9 9 5 7 4 2 3 0 2 *